Delicious Mediterranean Diet Snacks Recipes Cookbook

← ─────────────────────────── →

Tasty Bites Simple Steps Colorful Photos

By Zoe Rivers

Copyright © by Zoe Rivers

This cookbook brings you a collection of flavorful Mediterranean snacks that are as healthy as they are delicious. Delicious Mediterranean Diet Snacks Recipes Cookbook offers a variety of mouthwatering snack recipes with simple steps and vibrant photos, helping you enjoy the benefits of the Mediterranean diet.

Thank you for choosing Delicious Mediterranean Diet Snacks Recipes Cookbook. We hope it inspires you to try new, healthy snack options that align with your lifestyle and health goals!

Introduction

Welcome to Delicious Mediterranean Diet Snacks Recipes Cookbook: Tasty Bites, Simple Steps, Colorful Photos! This cookbook is your perfect guide to creating healthy, flavorful Mediterranean snacks that are easy to prepare and packed with authentic, delicious ingredients. Whether you're new to the Mediterranean diet or a seasoned fan, this book will help you enjoy the benefits of this healthy, vibrant lifestyle with every bite.

Why You'll Love This Cookbook

Eating healthy doesn't have to be complicated. Delicious Mediterranean Diet Snacks offers a wide range of snack recipes that are as simple to make as they are tasty. From savory treats to sweet indulgences, each recipe is crafted with fresh, wholesome ingredients that bring the flavors of the Mediterranean to your table. You'll love how quick and easy it is to create delicious, nutritious snacks without spending hours in the kitchen.

What's Inside?

The book is divided into 5 chapters, each featuring 10 unique recipes to satisfy your cravings and fuel your day:

- ✓ **50 Authentic Recipes**: A variety of Mediterranean-inspired snacks, perfect for every occasion.
- ✓ **5 Chapters**:
  - ✓ **Classic Mediterranean Bites**: Timeless, savory snacks.
  - ✓ **Crunchy & Nutty Treats**: Delightful textures and flavors.
  - ✓ **Vegetable Delights**: Healthy, veggie-packed options.
  - ✓ **Sea-Inspired Snacks**: Fresh, seafood-based recipes.
  - ✓ **Sweet Mediterranean Treats**: Delicious, guilt-free desserts.

Key Features:

- ✓ **Original, Colorful Photos**: Every recipe is accompanied by a beautiful photo.
- ✓ **Easy-to-Follow Instructions**: Simple, step-by-step directions for success.
- ✓ **Perfect Flavors**: Carefully tested recipes that offer the ideal balance of taste and health.
- ✓ **No Grammar or Spelling Errors**: Professionally proofread for an easy reading experience.

Start enjoying Mediterranean snacks today with Delicious Mediterranean Diet Snacks Recipes Cookbook!

Table of Contents

Chapter 01: Classic Mediterranean Bites

Recipe 01: Mediterranean Stuffed Naan

Mediterranean stuffed naan calzone quesadillas paired with mayo fries, peri bites, and chicken strips are a flavorful snack for gatherings or indulgent treats. This classic Mediterranean diet-inspired bites recipe balances textures and flavors, leaving everyone craving more.

Servings: 4

Prepping Time: 20 minutes

Cook Time: 25 minutes

Difficulty: Moderate

Ingredients:

- ✓ 4 naan bread pieces
- ✓ 2 cups shredded mozzarella cheese
- ✓ 1 cup cooked, shredded chicken
- ✓ 1/2 cup chopped spinach
- ✓ 1/4 cup diced olives
- ✓ 1/4 cup sun-dried tomatoes, chopped
- ✓ 1/4 teaspoon oregano
- ✓ 1/4 teaspoon paprika
- ✓ 1/4 cup mayonnaise
- ✓ 2 large potatoes, sliced into fries
- ✓ 4 peri bites or green chilies stuffed with cheese
- ✓ 1 cup breaded chicken strips, cooked
- ✓ 2 tablespoons olive oil

Step-by-Step Preparation:

1. Preheat a skillet over medium heat and brush it with olive oil.
2. Combine chicken, spinach, olives, sun-dried tomatoes, oregano, and paprika in a bowl.
3. Place a naan on a flat surface, spread the chicken mixture, and sprinkle mozzarella on top. Fold into a calzone shape.
4. Cook the stuffed naan in the skillet for 2–3 minutes on each side until golden and cheese is melted.
5. Prepare fries by air-frying or deep-frying until crispy, then toss with mayonnaise.
6. Cook peri bites and chicken strips according to preference.
7. Serve the calzones with mayo fries, peri bites, and chicken strips.

Nutritional Facts: (Per serving)

- ❖ Calories: 430
- ❖ Protein: 25g
- ❖ Carbohydrates: 40g
- ❖ Fat: 15g
- ❖ Fiber: 4g

This delicious and filling Mediterranean snack platter will satisfy your cravings. Pair it with your favorite dipping sauces for a complete flavor experience!

Recipe 02: Freshly Baked Turkish Borek

Golden and flaky, Turkish Börek is a Mediterranean classic filled with creamy cheese and baked to perfection in an oven tray. Perfect for snack time, gatherings, or traditional food presentations, this delightful recipe offers the authentic taste of Turkish cuisine with every bite.

Servings: 6

Prepping Time: 20 minutes

Cook Time: 40 minutes

Difficulty: Moderate

Ingredients:

- ✓ 1 package phyllo pastry (12 sheets)
- ✓ 1 cup feta cheese, crumbled
- ✓ 1/2 cup ricotta cheese
- ✓ 1/4 cup chopped parsley
- ✓ 2 eggs
- ✓ 1 cup milk
- ✓ 1/4 cup olive oil
- ✓ 1/2 teaspoon salt
- ✓ 1/2 teaspoon black pepper
- ✓ Sesame seeds for garnish

Step-by-Step Preparation:

1. Preheat the oven to 375°F (190°C). Grease a large oven tray with olive oil.
2. In a bowl, mix feta, ricotta, parsley, salt, and pepper to make the filling.
3. In another bowl, whisk together eggs, milk, and olive oil for the pastry wash.
4. Layer a sheet of phyllo on the tray, brush with the egg mixture, and repeat with 6 sheets.
5. Spread the cheese filling evenly over the layered phyllo.
6. Layer the remaining phyllo sheets on top, brushing each with the egg mixture.
7. Sprinkle sesame seeds over the top layer.
8. Bake for 35–40 minutes or until golden and crisp.
9. Let the börek cool slightly before slicing into squares or triangles for serving.

Nutritional Facts: (Per serving)

- ❖ Calories: 310
- ❖ Protein: 12g
- ❖ Carbohydrates: 25g
- ❖ Fat: 18g
- ❖ Fiber: 2g

Crispy, cheesy, and packed with flavor, this Turkish Börek is a versatile snack for any occasion. Serve it warm with a side of fresh Mediterranean salad for an unforgettable meal experience.

Recipe 03: Cod Fritters

Crispy on the outside, and tender on the inside, these traditional Spanish Cod Fritters, or Buñuelos de Bacalao, are a delicious snack with Mediterranean flair. Perfect as tapas or appetizers, they offer a perfect balance of flavors and textures, making them a popular choice for gatherings or a flavorful Mediterranean-inspired meal.

Servings: 4

Prepping Time: 15 minutes

Cook Time: 10 minutes

Difficulty: Easy

Ingredients:

- ✓ 1/2 lb salt cod, soaked and flaked
- ✓ 1/2 cup all-purpose flour
- ✓ 1/4 cup breadcrumbs
- ✓ 1/4 teaspoon baking powder
- ✓ 1/4 cup finely chopped parsley
- ✓ 2 cloves garlic, minced
- ✓ 1/2 cup warm water
- ✓ 1 egg
- ✓ Salt and pepper to taste
- ✓ Olive oil for frying

Step-by-Step Preparation:

1. Soak the salt cod for 24 hours, changing the water a few times.
2. Flake the cod and set it aside.
3. In a bowl, mix the flour, breadcrumbs, baking powder, parsley, garlic, salt, and pepper.
4. Add the egg and warm water to form a thick batter.
5. Fold in the flaked cod and mix until evenly combined.
6. Heat olive oil in a skillet over medium-high heat.
7. Drop spoonfuls of the batter into the hot oil, frying for 3-4 minutes on each side until golden and crispy.
8. Drain the fritters on paper towels.

Nutritional Facts: (Per serving)

- ❖ Calories: 220
- ❖ Protein: 15g
- ❖ Carbohydrates: 18g
- ❖ Fat: 12g
- ❖ Fiber: 1g

Serve your Buñuelos de Bacalao hot with a squeeze of lemon and a side of fresh salad. These crispy cod fritters bring a taste of Spain to your table, perfect for sharing with friends or family.

Recipe 04: Spanish Ham Croquettes

These classic Spanish ham croquettes are a delicious blend of high-quality jamón and velvety béchamel sauce, coated in crispy breadcrumbs. This Mediterranean snack is the perfect combination of creamy and crunchy, making it an irresistible bite for any occasion.

Servings: 6

Prepping Time: 30 minutes

Cook Time: 10 minutes

Difficulty: Moderate

Ingredients:

- ✓ 1/2 lb jamón serrano, finely chopped
- ✓ 1 cup milk
- ✓ 2 tablespoons butter
- ✓ 2 tablespoons all-purpose flour
- ✓ 1/4 teaspoon nutmeg
- ✓ 1/4 teaspoon black pepper
- ✓ 1 egg, beaten
- ✓ 1 cup breadcrumbs
- ✓ Olive oil for frying
- ✓ Salt to taste

Step-by-Step Preparation:

1. In a pan, melt butter over medium heat, then whisk in flour and cook for 1–2 minutes.
2. Slowly add milk, stirring constantly until the mixture thickens into a smooth béchamel sauce.
3. Stir in the jamón, nutmeg, and black pepper. Cook for an additional 2 minutes.
4. Transfer the mixture to a bowl, cover, and chill for 2–3 hours.
5. Shape the mixture into small croquettes.
6. Dip each croquette into the beaten egg and coat with breadcrumbs.
7. Heat olive oil in a skillet over medium-high heat and fry the croquettes until golden brown, about 3–4 minutes per side.
8. Drain on paper towels.

Nutritional Facts: (Per serving)

- ❖ Calories: 250
- ❖ Protein: 14g
- ❖ Carbohydrates: 18g
- ❖ Fat: 15g
- ❖ Fiber: 1g

Serve these golden, crispy croquettes as an appetizer or snack, with a side of aioli or a fresh green salad for a taste of Spain right at your table.

Recipe 05: Lasagna Made With Minced Beef Bolognese

This classic lasagna made with minced beef bolognese is a hearty Mediterranean dish that layers rich, flavorful meat sauce with creamy cheese and pasta. Perfect for family dinners or gatherings, it's a satisfying and timeless recipe that will warm hearts and bellies.

Servings: 6

Prepping Time: 20 minutes

Cook Time: 40 minutes

Difficulty: Moderate

Ingredients:

- ✓ 1 lb minced beef
- ✓ 1 onion, finely chopped
- ✓ 2 cloves garlic, minced
- ✓ 1 can (14 oz) crushed tomatoes
- ✓ 2 tablespoons tomato paste
- ✓ 1/2 cup red wine (optional)
- ✓ 1 teaspoon dried oregano
- ✓ 1 teaspoon dried basil
- ✓ 9 lasagna noodles, cooked
- ✓ 2 cups ricotta cheese
- ✓ 2 cups shredded mozzarella cheese
- ✓ 1/2 cup grated Parmesan cheese
- ✓ Salt and pepper to taste

Step-by-Step Preparation:

1. In a large skillet, brown the minced beef over medium heat. Add onion and garlic and cook until softened.
2. Stir in crushed tomatoes, tomato paste, red wine (if using), oregano, basil, salt, and pepper. Simmer for 15-20 minutes to thicken the sauce.
3. Preheat the oven to 375°F (190°C).
4. In a baking dish, layer lasagna noodles, followed by the bolognese sauce, ricotta, mozzarella, and Parmesan. Repeat the layers, ending with a layer of cheese on top.
5. Cover with foil and bake for 25 minutes.
6. Remove the foil and bake for an additional 10-15 minutes until bubbly and golden.
7. Let the lasagna cool for 5-10 minutes before serving.

Nutritional Facts: (Per serving)

- ❖ Calories: 450
- ❖ Protein: 30g
- ❖ Carbohydrates: 35g
- ❖ Fat: 25g
- ❖ Fiber: 4g

Serve this rich and comforting lasagna with a side of fresh salad and crusty bread for a complete meal. A true Mediterranean delight that's perfect for any occasion!

Recipe 06: Turkish Fish Sandwich

Balık Ekmek, a beloved Turkish fish sandwich, combines perfectly grilled fish with fresh vegetables and soft bread for an iconic Mediterranean street food experience. This classic recipe is quick, healthy, and bursting with authentic flavors that transport you straight to the streets of Istanbul.

Servings: 4

Prepping Time: 15 minutes

Cook Time: 15 minutes

Difficulty: Easy

Ingredients:

- ✓ 4 fillets of mackerel or other firm white fish
- ✓ 4 Turkish bread rolls or crusty baguettes
- ✓ 1 tablespoon olive oil
- ✓ 1 teaspoon paprika
- ✓ 1 teaspoon dried oregano
- ✓ Salt and pepper to taste
- ✓ 1 red onion, thinly sliced
- ✓ 1 cup shredded lettuce
- ✓ 1 tomato, thinly sliced
- ✓ 1 lemon, cut into wedges
- ✓ Optional: 1/4 cup mayonnaise or yogurt sauce

Step-by-Step Preparation:

1. Preheat a grill pan over medium-high heat and brush it with olive oil.
2. Season the fish fillets with paprika, oregano, salt, and pepper.
3. Grill the fish for 3–4 minutes per side until cooked through and slightly charred.
4. Lightly toast the bread rolls or baguettes.
5. Assemble the sandwich by layering lettuce, tomato, and onion on the bread.
6. Place the grilled fish on top and add a drizzle of mayonnaise or yogurt sauce if desired.
7. Serve with lemon wedges on the side for an extra burst of freshness.

Nutritional Facts: (Per serving)

- ❖ Calories: 320
- ❖ Protein: 25g
- ❖ Carbohydrates: 28g
- ❖ Fat: 12g
- ❖ Fiber: 3g

Balık Ekmek is a quick and satisfying Mediterranean bite, perfect for lunch or a light dinner. Pair it with a side of olives or a fresh cucumber salad for a complete and authentic meal.

Recipe 07: Skewer of Spanish Omelette With Bread

A skewer of Spanish omelet with bread is a delightful Mediterranean bite, combining the richness of a traditional Spanish tortilla with crispy bread for a satisfying snack or appetizer. This easy recipe brings together simple ingredients to create a savory, portable dish perfect for sharing.

Servings: 4

Prepping Time: 15 minutes

Cook Time: 20 minutes

Difficulty: Easy

Ingredients:

- ✓ 4 large eggs
- ✓ 2 medium potatoes, peeled and thinly sliced
- ✓ 1 small onion, finely chopped
- ✓ 1 tablespoon olive oil
- ✓ 4 slices of crusty bread
- ✓ Salt and pepper to taste
- ✓ Fresh parsley for garnish

Step-by-Step Preparation:

1. Heat olive oil in a large skillet over medium heat. Add the potatoes and onions, cooking until soft and golden, about 10 minutes.
2. Beat the eggs in a bowl and season with salt and pepper.
3. Add the cooked potatoes and onions to the beaten eggs, mixing gently.
4. Pour the mixture back into the skillet and cook over low heat until set about 10 minutes. Flip to cook the other side if needed.
5. Slice the omelet into small squares or rectangles.
6. Toast the slices of bread and cut them into smaller pieces.
7. Skewer the bread and omelet pieces alternately, securing them with toothpicks or small skewers.
8. Garnish with fresh parsley and serve warm.

Nutritional Facts: (Per serving)

- ❖ Calories: 280
- ❖ Protein: 12g
- ❖ Carbohydrates: 35g
- ❖ Fat: 14g
- ❖ Fiber: 3g

This Spanish omelet skewer with bread offers a fun twist on a classic dish. Enjoy it as an appetizer or a savory snack, paired with a glass of wine for a true Mediterranean experience!

Recipe 08: Baked Pizza With Golden Crust

This baked pizza with a golden crust, topped with savory ham, earthy champignons, and melted cheese, is a delicious Mediterranean-inspired snack or meal. Perfectly balanced in flavors, it offers a comforting bite that's both hearty and satisfying. Ideal for lunch or dinner, this easy recipe is sure to please everyone at the table.

Servings: 4

Prepping Time: 15 minutes

Cook Time: 20 minutes

Difficulty: Easy

Ingredients:

- ✓ 1 pizza dough (store-bought or homemade)
- ✓ 1/2 cup tomato sauce
- ✓ 1/2 cup grated mozzarella cheese
- ✓ 1/2 cup sliced ham
- ✓ 1/2 cup sliced champignons (mushrooms)
- ✓ 1 tablespoon olive oil
- ✓ Salt and pepper to taste
- ✓ Fresh oregano or basil for garnish

Step-by-Step Preparation:

1. Preheat the oven to 475°F (245°C).
2. Roll out the pizza dough on a lightly floured surface to your desired thickness.
3. Spread tomato sauce evenly on the dough, leaving a small border around the edges.
4. Top with grated mozzarella cheese, ham slices, and sliced champignons.
5. Drizzle olive oil over the top and season with salt and pepper.
6. Bake the pizza for 15–20 minutes, or until the crust is golden and the cheese is bubbly.
7. Remove from the oven, garnish with fresh oregano or basil, and slice.

Nutritional Facts: (Per serving)

- ❖ Calories: 350
- ❖ Protein: 20g
- ❖ Carbohydrates: 40g
- ❖ Fat: 15g
- ❖ Fiber: 2g

This baked pizza is the perfect combination of crispy, cheesy, and savory. Serve with a side of salad or enjoy it on its own for a fulfilling Mediterranean-inspired meal.

Recipe 09: Mozzarella Cheese With Tomatoes and Olives

This simple yet flavorful mozzarella cheese with tomatoes and olives is a classic Mediterranean snack that highlights the freshness of quality ingredients. Light, healthy, and bursting with taste, it's the perfect appetizer or side dish to accompany any meal.

Servings: 4

Prepping Time: 10 minutes

Cook Time: 0 minutes

Difficulty: Easy

Ingredients:

- ✓ 8 oz fresh mozzarella cheese, sliced
- ✓ 2 medium tomatoes, sliced
- ✓ 1/4 cup Kalamata olives, pitted and halved
- ✓ 1 tablespoon extra virgin olive oil
- ✓ 1 tablespoon balsamic vinegar
- ✓ Fresh basil leaves for garnish
- ✓ Salt and pepper to taste

Step-by-Step Preparation:

1. Arrange the mozzarella slices, tomato slices, and olives on a serving platter.
2. Drizzle with extra virgin olive oil and balsamic vinegar.
3. Season with salt and pepper to taste.
4. Garnish with fresh basil leaves.
5. Serve immediately or chill for 10 minutes before serving.

Nutritional Facts: (Per serving)

- ❖ Calories: 250
- ❖ Protein: 12g
- ❖ Carbohydrates: 8g
- ❖ Fat: 20g
- ❖ Fiber: 2g

This mozzarella, tomato, and olive dish is a light and refreshing Mediterranean treat, perfect for warm days or as a flavorful appetizer before a main course. Enjoy with a glass of crisp white wine for an authentic Mediterranean experience.

Recipe 10: Homemade Twisted Pizza Rolls

These homemade twisted pizza rolls are a fun, bite-sized version of your favorite pizza. Filled with tomato sauce, fresh tomatoes, and melted cheese, they're a trendy and delicious finger food, perfect for snacking, parties, or casual meals. Easy to make, they bring all the flavors of pizza in a fun, portable form.

Servings: 4

Cook Time: 20 minutes

Prepping Time: 15 minutes

Difficulty: Easy

Ingredients:

- ✓ 1 pizza dough (store-bought or homemade)
- ✓ 1/2 cup tomato sauce
- ✓ 1 cup shredded mozzarella cheese
- ✓ 1 medium tomato, diced
- ✓ 1/2 teaspoon dried oregano
- ✓ 1/2 teaspoon garlic powder
- ✓ Olive oil for brushing
- ✓ Salt and pepper to taste

Step-by-Step Preparation:

1. Preheat the oven to 375°F (190°C).
2. Roll out the pizza dough into a rectangular shape.
3. Spread a thin layer of tomato sauce over the dough, leaving a small border around the edges.
4. Sprinkle with shredded mozzarella, diced tomato, oregano, and garlic powder.
5. Carefully roll up the dough into a log and slice it into 1-inch rolls.
6. Place the rolls on a greased baking sheet, brush with olive oil, and season with salt and pepper.
7. Bake for 18-20 minutes or until golden and bubbly.

Nutritional Facts: (Per serving)

- ❖ Calories: 280
- ❖ Protein: 12g
- ❖ Carbohydrates: 32g
- ❖ Fat: 14g
- ❖ Fiber: 2g

These twisted pizza rolls are a crowd-pleaser, perfect for any gathering or a quick snack. Serve with extra tomato sauce for dipping, and enjoy this Mediterranean-inspired twist on pizza!

Chapter 02: Crunchy & Nutty Treats

Recipe 11: Fried Bread With Olive Oil

Fried bread with olive oil, garlic, and herbs is a Mediterranean-inspired snack that's simple yet bursting with flavor. The crispy bread, infused with aromatic garlic and herbs, makes for a delightful crunchy, and nutty treat. Perfect for an afternoon snack or appetizer to impress your guests.

Servings: 4

Prepping Time: 5 minutes

Cook Time: 10 minutes

Difficulty: Easy

Ingredients:

- ✓ 4 slices of rustic bread (day-old works best)
- ✓ 3 tablespoons extra-virgin olive oil
- ✓ 2 garlic cloves, finely minced
- ✓ 1 teaspoon dried oregano
- ✓ 1 teaspoon dried thyme
- ✓ 1 teaspoon parsley (fresh or dried)
- ✓ A pinch of sea salt
- ✓ A pinch of freshly ground black pepper

Step-by-Step Preparation:

1. Heat a large skillet over medium heat and add the olive oil.
2. Once the oil is warm, toss in the minced garlic and sauté until fragrant, about 30 seconds.
3. Place the bread slices in the skillet and press down lightly with a spatula.
4. Sprinkle the oregano, thyme, parsley, salt, and pepper evenly over the bread slices.
5. Cook each side for 3-4 minutes until golden and crispy.
6. Remove from heat and serve warm, optionally garnished with extra parsley.

Nutritional Facts: (Per serving):

- ❖ Calories: 140
- ❖ Protein: 3g
- ❖ Carbohydrates: 20g
- ❖ Fats: 6g
- ❖ Fiber: 2g

This Mediterranean treat is perfect for enjoying a moment of simplicity and crunch. Pair it with hummus or a fresh salad for a wholesome snack.

Recipe 12: Carrot Slice Baklava With Pistachios

Carrot Slice Baklava with Pistachios is a unique twist on the classic Mediterranean treat. The combination of tender carrots, crunchy pistachios, and flaky phyllo dough creates a dessert that's both sweet and satisfying. This delightful snack is perfect for those looking to indulge in a nutritious yet indulgent treat.

Servings: 12

Prepping Time: 20 minutes

Cook Time: 40 minutes

Difficulty: Medium

Ingredients:

- ✓ 3 medium carrots, grated
- ✓ 1 cup pistachios, chopped
- ✓ 12 sheets of phyllo dough
- ✓ 1/2 cup melted butter
- ✓ 1/2 cup honey
- ✓ 1/4 cup brown sugar
- ✓ 1 teaspoon ground cinnamon
- ✓ 1 teaspoon vanilla extract
- ✓ A pinch of salt

Step-by-Step Preparation:

1. Preheat the oven to 350°F (175°C).
2. In a bowl, combine grated carrots, chopped pistachios, cinnamon, vanilla extract, and a pinch of salt.
3. Brush a baking dish with melted butter and layer 6 sheets of phyllo dough, brushing each with butter.
4. Spread half of the carrot-pistachio mixture evenly over the phyllo dough.
5. Layer 6 more sheets of phyllo dough over the mixture, brushing each with butter.
6. Bake for 30-40 minutes or until golden and crisp.
7. In a small saucepan, heat honey and brown sugar until dissolved. Pour over the baklava once it's out of the oven.
8. Let it cool completely before slicing into squares.

Nutritional Facts: (Per serving):

- ❖ Calories: 180
- ❖ Protein: 4g
- ❖ Carbohydrates: 22g
- ❖ Fats: 10g
- ❖ Fiber: 3g

This carrot slice baklava offers a crunchy, nutty bite with the perfect balance of sweetness and richness. It's the perfect Mediterranean snack for special occasions or a healthy dessert.

Recipe 13: Sicilian Cannoli With Pistachio Filling

Sicilian Cannoli with Pistachio Filling is a delightful Mediterranean treat that brings together crispy, golden shells and a rich, creamy pistachio filling. This indulgent yet balanced dessert is a perfect way to enjoy the traditional flavors of Sicily with a nutty twist, making it an irresistible snack for any occasion.

Servings: 6

Prepping Time: 25 minutes

Cook Time: 15 minutes

Difficulty: Medium

Ingredients:

- ✓ 6 cannoli shells (store-bought or homemade)
- ✓ 1/2 cup pistachios, finely ground
- ✓ 1 cup ricotta cheese
- ✓ 1/2 cup mascarpone cheese
- ✓ 1/4 cup powdered sugar
- ✓ 1/2 teaspoon vanilla extract
- ✓ A pinch of salt
- ✓ Chopped pistachios (for garnish)

Step-by-Step Preparation:

1. In a medium bowl, combine ricotta cheese, mascarpone cheese, ground pistachios, powdered sugar, vanilla extract, and a pinch of salt. Mix until smooth and creamy.

2. Spoon the pistachio mixture into a piping bag.

3. Carefully fill the cannoli shells with the pistachio cream, ensuring they are packed evenly.

4. Garnish the ends of the filled cannoli with chopped pistachios for added crunch.

5. Serve immediately for the best texture, or refrigerate until ready to enjoy.

Nutritional Facts: (Per serving):

- ❖ Calories: 220
- ❖ Protein: 6g
- ❖ Carbohydrates: 26g
- ❖ Fats: 13g
- ❖ Fiber: 3g

This Sicilian Cannoli with Pistachio Filling combines a delicious mix of textures and flavors, making it the perfect treat for any Mediterranean-inspired gathering or dessert craving.

Recipe 14: Pecan Baklava Pastry

Pecan Baklava is a delightful Mediterranean treat, offering a crispy, golden exterior and a nutty, rich filling of pecans. This twist on the classic baklava combines the flakiness of filo dough with the earthy sweetness of pecans, creating a perfect balance of textures and flavors for a satisfying snack or dessert.

Servings: 12

Cook Time: 35 minutes

Prepping Time: 20 minutes

Difficulty: Medium

Ingredients:

- ✓ 16 sheets of filo dough
- ✓ 1 cup pecans, chopped
- ✓ 1/2 cup unsalted butter, melted
- ✓ 1/2 cup honey
- ✓ 1/4 cup granulated sugar
- ✓ 1 teaspoon ground cinnamon
- ✓ A pinch of salt
- ✓ 1/2 teaspoon vanilla extract

Step-by-Step Preparation:

1. Preheat the oven to 350°F (175°C).
2. Brush a baking dish with melted butter and layer 8 sheets of filo dough, brushing each with butter.
3. In a bowl, mix chopped pecans, cinnamon, salt, and sugar. Spread the mixture evenly over the filo dough.
4. Layer the remaining 8 sheets of filo dough on top, buttering each sheet as you go.
5. Cut the baklava into squares or diamond shapes before baking.
6. Bake for 30-35 minutes or until golden brown and crispy.
7. In a small saucepan, heat honey and vanilla until smooth. Drizzle the syrup over the hot baklava once it's out of the oven.
8. Let cool completely before serving.

Nutritional Facts: (Per serving):

- ❖ Calories: 210
- ❖ Protein: 3g
- ❖ Carbohydrates: 25g
- ❖ Fats: 12g
- ❖ Fiber: 2g

This pecan baklava is the perfect crunchy, nutty snack, offering a delicious Mediterranean twist on a classic favorite. It's ideal for special occasions or a sweet treat any time.

Recipe 15: Pistachio Dome With Whole Almond

Pistachio Dome with Whole Almond is a Mediterranean-inspired treat that combines the rich crunch of pistachios with the smooth sweetness of almonds. This unique dessert features a perfect balance of textures, with each bite offering a delightful mix of nutty flavors. It's an indulgent yet wholesome snack, ideal for those seeking a crunchy, satisfying treat.

Servings: 8

Prepping Time: 20 minutes

Cook Time: 15 minutes

Difficulty: Medium

Ingredients:

- ✓ 1 cup pistachios, shelled and chopped
- ✓ 1/2 cup whole almonds
- ✓ 1/2 cup honey
- ✓ 1/4 cup coconut flour
- ✓ 1/4 cup almond flour
- ✓ 1/4 teaspoon vanilla extract
- ✓ 1 tablespoon coconut oil

Step-by-Step Preparation:

1. Preheat the oven to 350°F (175°C).
2. In a food processor, pulse pistachios, coconut flour, and almond flour until finely ground.
3. In a saucepan, heat honey and coconut oil over medium heat until melted.
4. Add the vanilla extract to the honey mixture, then combine it with the ground pistachios and almond flour. Stir until a dough forms.
5. Shape the mixture into small domes on a baking sheet lined with parchment paper. Press one whole almond into the center of each dome.
6. Bake for 12-15 minutes or until golden and firm.
7. Let cool completely before serving.

Nutritional Facts: (Per serving):

- ❖ Calories: 180
- ❖ Protein: 5g
- ❖ Carbohydrates: 14g
- ❖ Fats: 13g
- ❖ Fiber: 3g

These Pistachio Domes with Whole almonds are perfect for satisfying your snack cravings while enjoying the delightful flavors of the Mediterranean. Great for a crunchy bite any time of day!

Recipe 16: Small Wheat Tortillas

Pita Chips Pile is a perfect Mediterranean snack made with small wheat tortillas. These crispy, crunchy flatbreads are seasoned with a blend of herbs and spices, creating a flavorful, spicy bite that's satisfying yet light. A healthy, easy-to-make treat that's perfect for snacking, dipping, or serving at your next gathering.

Servings: 4

Cook Time: 15 minutes

Prepping Time: 10 minutes

Difficulty: Easy

Ingredients:

- ✓ 4 small wheat tortillas
- ✓ 2 tablespoons olive oil
- ✓ 1 teaspoon garlic powder
- ✓ 1 teaspoon dried oregano
- ✓ 1/2 teaspoon paprika
- ✓ 1/4 teaspoon cayenne pepper
- ✓ Salt to taste

Step-by-Step Preparation:

1. Preheat the oven to 375°F (190°C).
2. Brush both sides of the tortillas with olive oil.
3. Stack the tortillas and cut them into triangle wedges.
4. In a small bowl, mix garlic powder, oregano, paprika, cayenne pepper, and salt. Sprinkle the seasoning over the tortilla wedges.
5. Place the wedges in a single layer on a baking sheet.
6. Bake for 10-15 minutes or until golden and crispy.
7. Allow to cool before serving.

Nutritional Facts: (Per serving):

- ❖ Calories: 140
- ❖ Protein: 3g
- ❖ Carbohydrates: 18g
- ❖ Fats: 7g
- ❖ Fiber: 3g

These Pita Chips Pile are the ultimate Mediterranean crunchy snack, perfect for dipping into your favorite hummus or yogurt sauce. Simple, quick, and full of flavor!

Recipe 17: Hot Breaded Calamari Strips

Hot breaded calamari strips served with lemon wedges are a Mediterranean-inspired treat that brings crispy, golden calamari to life. The delicate squid strips, coated in seasoned breadcrumbs, are fried to perfection and paired with zesty lemon, offering a delightful balance of crunch and freshness. Perfect as an appetizer or a savory snack.

Servings: 4

Prepping Time: 15 minutes

Cook Time: 5 minutes

Difficulty: Easy

Ingredients:

- ✓ 1 lb calamari rings (fresh or thawed)
- ✓ 1/2 cup all-purpose flour
- ✓ 1/2 cup breadcrumbs
- ✓ 1 teaspoon garlic powder
- ✓ 1 teaspoon paprika
- ✓ 1/2 teaspoon salt
- ✓ 1/4 teaspoon black pepper
- ✓ 2 eggs, beaten
- ✓ Olive oil for frying
- ✓ Lemon wedges for serving

Step-by-Step Preparation:

1. Heat olive oil in a deep skillet or frying pan over medium-high heat.
2. In one bowl, combine flour, breadcrumbs, garlic powder, paprika, salt, and pepper.
3. In a separate bowl, beat the eggs.
4. Dip each calamari ring into the egg mixture, then coat in the breadcrumb mixture.
5. Fry the calamari strips in hot oil for 2-3 minutes, or until golden and crispy.
6. Remove from the oil and drain on paper towels.
7. Serve immediately with lemon wedges.

Nutritional Facts: (Per serving):

- ❖ Calories: 220
- ❖ Protein: 14g
- ❖ Carbohydrates: 18g
- ❖ Fats: 12g
- ❖ Fiber: 1g

These crispy breaded calamari strips are an irresistible Mediterranean snack, offering the perfect blend of crunchy texture and refreshing lemon. A delicious and satisfying treat to enjoy with friends or family!

Recipe 18: Italian Grissini Bread Sticks

Italian grissini breadsticks with sesame seeds are a classic Mediterranean snack, offering a crunchy, nutty flavor in every bite. These thin, crisp sticks are perfect for dipping or serving alongside your favorite antipasto platter. With the addition of sesame seeds, they add a delightful texture and a subtle nuttiness that makes them irresistible.

Servings: 6

Prepping Time: 15 minutes

Cook Time: 25 minutes

Difficulty: Easy

Ingredients:

- ✓ 1 cup all-purpose flour
- ✓ 1/2 cup warm water
- ✓ 1 tablespoon olive oil
- ✓ 1 teaspoon active dry yeast
- ✓ 1/2 teaspoon salt
- ✓ 1 tablespoon sugar
- ✓ 2 tablespoons sesame seeds

Step-by-Step Preparation:

1. In a bowl, dissolve sugar and yeast in warm water. Let sit for 5 minutes until foamy.
2. In a mixing bowl, combine flour and salt. Add olive oil and the yeast mixture, mixing until a dough forms.
3. Knead the dough on a floured surface for about 5 minutes until smooth.
4. Cover the dough and let it rise for 1 hour, or until doubled in size.
5. Preheat the oven to 375°F (190°C).
6. Roll the dough into long, thin strips (about 8 inches).
7. Brush the breadsticks with a little olive oil and sprinkle with sesame seeds.
8. Place the sticks on a baking sheet and bake for 20-25 minutes or until golden brown and crispy.
9. Let cool before serving.

Nutritional Facts: (Per serving):

- ❖ Calories: 120
- ❖ Protein: 3g
- ❖ Carbohydrates: 20g
- ❖ Fats: 4g
- ❖ Fiber: 1g

These grissini breadsticks are an irresistible Mediterranean snack, perfect for pairing with dips or enjoying on their own. Their crunchy texture and nutty flavor make them a delightful addition to any meal or gathering.

Recipe 19: Semolina Cookies

Semolina cookies are a delightful Mediterranean treat with a crunchy texture and a subtle nutty flavor, thanks to the use of semolina flour. These cookies are perfect for those who enjoy a lighter, crispy snack that pairs wonderfully with tea or coffee. Simple to make and full of flavor, they're a great addition to any dessert spread.

Servings: 12

Prepping Time: 15 minutes

Cook Time: 20 minutes

Difficulty: Easy

Ingredients:

- ✓ 1 cup semolina flour
- ✓ 1/2 cup all-purpose flour
- ✓ 1/2 cup unsalted butter, softened
- ✓ 1/4 cup sugar
- ✓ 1 teaspoon vanilla extract
- ✓ 1/4 teaspoon baking powder
- ✓ A pinch of salt
- ✓ 1 egg

Step-by-Step Preparation:

1. Preheat the oven to 350°F (175°C) and line a baking sheet with parchment paper.
2. In a bowl, combine semolina flour, all-purpose flour, baking powder, and salt.
3. In another bowl, beat the butter and sugar until light and creamy.
4. Add the egg and vanilla extract to the butter mixture and mix well.
5. Gradually incorporate the dry ingredients into the wet ingredients, mixing until a dough forms.
6. Roll the dough into small balls and flatten them slightly with your hands.
7. Place the cookies on the prepared baking sheet, leaving space between each.
8. Bake for 18-20 minutes, or until the cookies are golden brown around the edges.
9. Let cool before serving.

Nutritional Facts: (Per serving):

- ❖ Calories: 150
- ❖ Protein: 2g
- ❖ Carbohydrates: 20g
- ❖ Fats: 8g
- ❖ Fiber: 1g

These semolina cookies are the perfect balance of crunch and flavor, offering a light and nutty treat. Enjoy them with a cup of tea or coffee for an authentic Mediterranean snack experience!

Recipe 20: Almond-Crusted Fish

Almond-crusted fish offers a delightful Mediterranean twist on a healthy, flavorful meal. The delicate fish fillet is coated with a crispy almond crust, providing a perfect crunch while maintaining a light and tender interior. Paired with roasted vegetables, this dish is a delicious, nutritious, and satisfying option for any meal.

Servings: 4

Prepping Time: 15 minutes

Cook Time: 20 minutes

Difficulty: Easy

Ingredients:

- ✓ 4 fish fillets (such as cod or tilapia)
- ✓ 1 cup almond meal
- ✓ 1/4 cup breadcrumbs
- ✓ 1 egg, beaten
- ✓ 1 teaspoon dried oregano
- ✓ 1/2 teaspoon garlic powder
- ✓ Salt and pepper to taste
- ✓ Olive oil for drizzling
- ✓ 2 cups mixed vegetables (e.g., zucchini, bell peppers, carrots)

Step-by-Step Preparation:

1. Preheat the oven to 375°F (190°C).
2. In a shallow dish, combine almond meal, breadcrumbs, oregano, garlic powder, salt, and pepper.
3. Dip each fish fillet in the beaten egg, then coat evenly with the almond mixture.
4. Place the fish fillets on a baking sheet lined with parchment paper and drizzle with olive oil.
5. Arrange the mixed vegetables on the same sheet, drizzle with olive oil, and season with salt and pepper.
6. Bake for 15-20 minutes, until the fish is golden and the vegetables are tender.
7. Serve hot with a side of roasted vegetables.

Nutritional Facts: (Per serving):

- ❖ Calories: 350
- ❖ Protein: 30g
- ❖ Carbohydrates: 12g
- ❖ Fats: 20g
- ❖ Fiber: 4g

Almond-crusted fish is a perfect combination of crunchy texture and delicate fish, offering a wholesome Mediterranean meal. Served with roasted vegetables, it's a light yet filling dish, packed with flavor and nutrients.

Chapter 03: Vegetable Delights

Recipe 21: Vegetable Vegan Pie

A savory Mediterranean-inspired vegetable pie, this fresh-baked galette combines the richness of olives, zucchini, tomatoes, and asparagus, all seasoned with fragrant spices and olive oil. Perfect for a quick snack or a light meal, this vegan delight bursts with flavor and offers a satisfying crunch.

Servings: 4

Prepping Time: 15 minutes

Cook Time: 30 minutes

Difficulty: Easy

Ingredients:

- ✓ 1 sheet of vegan puff pastry
- ✓ 1/2 cup pitted black olives, chopped
- ✓ 1 zucchini, sliced
- ✓ 1 medium tomato, sliced
- ✓ 6-8 asparagus spears, trimmed and chopped
- ✓ 1 tbsp olive oil
- ✓ 1 tsp dried oregano
- ✓ 1/2 tsp garlic powder
- ✓ Salt and pepper to taste

Step-by-Step Preparation:

1. Preheat oven to 375°F (190°C).
2. Roll out the puff pastry on a baking sheet.
3. Layer sliced zucchini, tomatoes, and asparagus in the center, leaving a border around the edges.
4. Sprinkle with chopped olives, oregano, garlic powder, salt, and pepper.
5. Drizzle with olive oil.
6. Fold the edges of the pastry over the vegetables, creating a rustic galette shape.
7. Bake for 25-30 minutes or until golden and crisp.

Nutritional Facts: (Per serving)

- ❖ Calories: 250
- ❖ Fat: 18g
- ❖ Carbohydrates: 22g
- ❖ Fiber: 3g
- ❖ Protein: 4g

This vegetable galette is a delightful and healthy snack that's as satisfying as it is delicious. The combination of fresh vegetables and spices creates a perfect balance, and the golden crust adds a delightful crunch. Enjoy this Mediterranean-inspired treat as a midday snack or light dinner!

Recipe 22: Roasted Eggplant Hummus

A creamy and smoky roasted eggplant hummus, paired with briny olives, crunchy pickled cucumbers, and crispy croutons, makes for the perfect Mediterranean snack. This flavorful dip is simple to prepare yet packed with rich, savory flavors. It's a healthy and satisfying way to enjoy a light bite that transports you to the Mediterranean coast.

Servings: 4

Cook Time: 25 minutes

Prepping Time: 15 minutes

Difficulty: Easy

Ingredients:

- ✓ 1 medium eggplant
- ✓ 1/2 cup tahini
- ✓ 2 tbsp olive oil
- ✓ 1 tbsp lemon juice
- ✓ 1 garlic clove, minced
- ✓ Salt and pepper to taste
- ✓ 1/4 cup pitted black olives
- ✓ 1/4 cup pickled cucumbers, sliced
- ✓ Croutons, for serving

Step-by-Step Preparation:

1. Preheat oven to 400°F (200°C).
2. Slice eggplant in half and roast on a baking sheet for 20-25 minutes until soft.
3. Scoop out the flesh of the eggplant and place it in a blender or food processor.
4. Add tahini, olive oil, lemon juice, garlic, salt, and pepper. Blend until smooth.
5. Transfer the hummus to a serving bowl.
6. Top with sliced olives, pickled cucumbers, and croutons. Serve immediately.

Nutritional Facts: (Per serving)

- ❖ Calories: 180
- ❖ Fat: 14g
- ❖ Carbohydrates: 15g
- ❖ Fiber: 5g
- ❖ Protein: 3g

This roasted eggplant hummus is a versatile, vibrant dip that pairs beautifully with Mediterranean sides. The blend of creamy eggplant, tahini, and tangy olives makes it an irresistible snack for any occasion. Enjoy it with a side of crunchy croutons for an added texture boost. A true Mediterranean delight!

Recipe 23: Pumpkin, Leek, Gorgonzola Cheese Crunchy Pie

This savory pumpkin, leek, and Gorgonzola cheese pie combines the earthy sweetness of pumpkin with the rich, tangy flavor of Gorgonzola. Wrapped in a golden, crispy crust, it's a Mediterranean-inspired treat that's perfect for a light lunch or a delightful snack. The combination of flavors creates a satisfying, crunchy pie that will become a new favorite.

Servings: 4

Prepping Time: 15 minutes

Cook Time: 35 minutes

Difficulty: Medium

Ingredients:

- ✓ 1 small pumpkin, peeled and diced
- ✓ 2 medium leeks, cleaned and sliced
- ✓ 1/2 cup crumbled Gorgonzola cheese
- ✓ 1 sheet puff pastry
- ✓ 2 tbsp olive oil
- ✓ 1 tbsp fresh thyme
- ✓ Salt and pepper to taste

Step-by-Step Preparation:

1. Preheat oven to 375°F (190°C).
2. Heat olive oil in a pan and sauté the leeks until soft, about 5-7 minutes.
3. Add diced pumpkin to the pan and cook until tender, about 10 minutes.
4. Season with thyme, salt, and pepper. Let the mixture cool.
5. Roll out the puff pastry and transfer it to a baking dish.
6. Fill with the pumpkin-leek mixture, then sprinkle Gorgonzola cheese on top.
7. Fold over the edges of the pastry and bake for 25-30 minutes until golden and crispy.

Nutritional Facts: (Per serving)

- ❖ Calories: 220
- ❖ Fat: 15g
- ❖ Carbohydrates: 18g
- ❖ Fiber: 4g
- ❖ Protein: 6g

This pumpkin, leek, and Gorgonzola pie is a unique twist on Mediterranean flavors. The combination of creamy cheese, roasted pumpkin, and sautéed leeks creates a perfect balance of savory and sweet. Enjoy it as a snack or appetizer, and savor the delightful crunch of this delicious pie. It's sure to impress!

Recipe 24: Golden Fried Stuffed Green Olives With Parmesan Cheese

These golden-fried stuffed green olives, filled with rich Parmesan cheese, offer a delightful Mediterranean snack. The crispy outer layer combined with the creamy, savory filling makes them the perfect bite-sized treat for any occasion. Quick to prepare and packed with flavor, they're sure to impress your guests or satisfy your cravings.

Servings: 4

Prepping Time: 10 minutes

Cook Time: 5 minutes

Difficulty: Easy

Ingredients:

- ✓ 12 green olives, pitted
- ✓ 1/4 cup grated Parmesan cheese
- ✓ 1/4 cup cream cheese
- ✓ 1/2 cup breadcrumbs
- ✓ 1/4 cup flour
- ✓ 1 egg, beaten
- ✓ Olive oil for frying
- ✓ Salt and pepper to taste

Step-by-Step Preparation:

1. In a bowl, mix Parmesan and cream cheese.
2. Stuff each pitted olive with the cheese mixture.
3. Roll stuffed olives in flour, then dip in beaten egg, and coat with breadcrumbs.
4. Heat olive oil in a pan over medium heat.
5. Fry olives for 2-3 minutes, or until golden brown.
6. Drain on paper towels and season with salt and pepper.

Nutritional Facts: (Per serving)

- ❖ Calories: 180
- ❖ Fat: 14g
- ❖ Carbohydrates: 10g
- ❖ Fiber: 1g
- ❖ Protein: 6g

These crispy, golden-fried stuffed olives with Parmesan are a Mediterranean snack at its best. The creamy cheese filling paired with the crunchy breadcrumb coating makes them irresistible. Serve them as an appetizer or a delightful party snack, and enjoy a bite of Mediterranean flavor in every crunchy, cheesy bite!

Recipe 25: Dry Crackers With Tomato and Basil

These simple yet flavorful dry crackers topped with fresh tomato and basil offer a perfect Mediterranean-inspired snack. The crunchy texture of the crackers is complemented by the juicy tomatoes and aromatic basil, creating a light, satisfying treat that is perfect for a quick snack or as an appetizer for your next gathering.

Servings: 4

Prepping Time: 10 minutes

Cook Time: 0 minutes

Difficulty: Easy

Ingredients:

- ✓ 12 dry crackers
- ✓ 2 ripe tomatoes, diced
- ✓ 1/4 cup fresh basil, chopped
- ✓ 1 tbsp olive oil
- ✓ Salt and pepper to taste
- ✓ Balsamic vinegar (optional)

Step-by-Step Preparation:

1. Arrange dry crackers on a serving plate.
2. In a bowl, combine diced tomatoes, chopped basil, olive oil, salt, and pepper.
3. Spoon the tomato-basil mixture onto each cracker.
4. Drizzle with balsamic vinegar, if desired.
5. Serve immediately and enjoy!

Nutritional Facts: (Per serving)

- ❖ Calories: 120
- ❖ Fat: 7g
- ❖ Carbohydrates: 15g
- ❖ Fiber: 2g
- ❖ Protein: 2g

These dry crackers with tomato and basil are a perfect light snack, bursting with fresh Mediterranean flavors. The combination of crunchy crackers, juicy tomatoes, and fragrant basil makes for an easy, yet delicious, treat. Perfect for a quick bite or a crowd-pleasing appetizer!

Recipe 26: Potato Fried Croquettes

These crispy potato-fried croquettes are the perfect Mediterranean snack, with a golden exterior and a soft, flavorful filling. Made with mashed potatoes, herbs, and spices, these croquettes are an irresistible treat that pairs well with dipping sauces or as an appetizer. Easy to prepare and packed with comforting flavors, they're a crowd-pleasing snack for any occasion.

Servings: 4

Prepping Time: 15 minutes

Cook Time: 10 minutes

Difficulty: Easy

Ingredients:

- ✓ 3 medium potatoes, boiled and mashed
- ✓ 1/4 cup grated Parmesan cheese
- ✓ 1/4 cup fresh parsley, chopped
- ✓ 1 egg, beaten
- ✓ 1/2 cup breadcrumbs
- ✓ Salt and pepper to taste
- ✓ Olive oil for frying

Step-by-Step Preparation:

1. In a bowl, combine mashed potatoes, Parmesan cheese, parsley, salt, and pepper.
2. Form the mixture into small oval-shaped croquettes.
3. Dip each croquette into the beaten egg, then coat it with breadcrumbs.
4. Heat olive oil in a frying pan over medium heat.
5. Fry the croquettes for 3-4 minutes on each side, or until golden brown.
6. Drain on paper towels and serve.

Nutritional Facts: (Per serving)

- ❖ Calories: 200
- ❖ Fat: 12g
- ❖ Carbohydrates: 22g
- ❖ Fiber: 3g
- ❖ Protein: 4g

These potato-fried croquettes are a delicious, crispy snack with the perfect blend of creamy potatoes and savory cheese. Perfect as a side dish, appetizer, or standalone snack, they're sure to be a hit at your next Mediterranean-inspired gathering. Enjoy the irresistible crunch and comforting flavor in every bite!

Recipe 27: Pull Apart Bread With Herbs

This homemade pull-apart bread is a warm, aromatic Mediterranean delight. Infused with fresh herbs like parsley, thyme, rosemary, and dill, combined with garlic, cheese, and spicy butter, it offers a burst of flavors in every bite. Perfect for gatherings or as a comforting snack, this pull-apart bread will surely become a crowd favorite.

Servings: 6

Prepping Time: 20 minutes

Cook Time: 30 minutes

Difficulty: Medium

Ingredients:

- ✓ 1 loaf of fresh bread dough
- ✓ 1/4 cup melted butter
- ✓ 3 cloves garlic, minced
- ✓ 1/4 cup grated cheese (Parmesan or mozzarella)
- ✓ 2 tbsp fresh parsley, chopped
- ✓ 1 tbsp fresh thyme, chopped
- ✓ 1 tbsp fresh rosemary, chopped
- ✓ 1 tbsp fresh dill, chopped
- ✓ 1/2 tsp chili flakes (optional)
- ✓ Salt and pepper to taste

Step-by-Step Preparation:

1. Preheat oven to 375°F (190°C).
2. Roll out the bread dough into a rectangle.
3. In a bowl, mix melted butter, garlic, herbs, cheese, chili flakes, salt, and pepper.
4. Spread the butter mixture evenly over the dough.
5. Slice the dough into strips, then stack and cut into squares.
6. Place the squares upright in a greased baking dish.
7. Bake for 25-30 minutes, until golden and bubbly.

Nutritional Facts: (Per serving)

- ❖ Calories: 250
- ❖ Fat: 18g
- ❖ Carbohydrates: 22g
- ❖ Fiber: 2g
- ❖ Protein: 6g

This pull-apart bread, loaded with garlic, herbs, and cheese, makes a perfect savory snack. The combination of fresh herbs and spicy butter creates a unique Mediterranean flavor that's both comforting and irresistible. Enjoy it fresh out of the oven for a delightful treat your family and friends will love!

Recipe 28: Bread With Homemade Pesto Sauce Spread

This simple yet delicious Mediterranean snack features fresh bread spread with homemade pesto sauce. The aromatic combination of basil, garlic, olive oil, and Parmesan creates a vibrant, savory flavor that perfectly complements crusty bread. Ideal for a quick snack or appetizer, this dish is easy to prepare and bursting with Mediterranean goodness.

Servings: 4

Cook Time: 0 minutes

Prepping Time: 10 minutes

Difficulty: Easy

Ingredients:

- ✓ 4 slices of fresh bread
- ✓ 1/4 cup fresh basil leaves
- ✓ 2 tbsp grated Parmesan cheese
- ✓ 2 tbsp olive oil
- ✓ 1 garlic clove
- ✓ Salt and pepper to taste

Step-by-Step Preparation:

1. In a blender or food processor, combine basil, Parmesan, olive oil, garlic, salt, and pepper.

2. Blend until smooth and creamy.

3. Toast bread slices lightly (optional).

4. Spread the homemade pesto sauce generously on each slice of bread using a knife.

5. Serve immediately and enjoy!

Nutritional Facts: (Per serving)

- ❖ Calories: 180
- ❖ Fat: 14g
- ❖ Carbohydrates: 12g
- ❖ Fiber: 2g
- ❖ Protein: 4g

This bread with homemade pesto spread is an easy yet flavorful Mediterranean snack. The fragrant pesto adds a burst of freshness, while the bread provides the perfect crunchy base. Enjoy this savory treat as a quick appetizer or a simple snack that embodies the flavors of the Mediterranean!

Recipe 29: Greek Cheese, Spinach Pie

This traditional homemade Greek cheese and spinach pie, also known as Spanakopita, is a delightful Mediterranean treat. The crispy, flaky phyllo dough encases a creamy mixture of spinach, feta cheese, and herbs, creating a savory snack perfect for any time of the day. It's a delicious and comforting dish that captures the essence of Greek cuisine.

Servings: 6

Prepping Time: 15 minutes

Cook Time: 35 minutes

Difficulty: Medium

Ingredients:

- ✓ 1 package phyllo dough
- ✓ 2 cups fresh spinach, chopped
- ✓ 1/2 cup feta cheese, crumbled
- ✓ 1/4 cup ricotta cheese
- ✓ 1 small onion, finely chopped
- ✓ 2 tbsp olive oil
- ✓ 1 egg, beaten
- ✓ Salt and pepper to taste

Step-by-Step Preparation:

1. Preheat oven to 375°F (190°C).

2. Sauté onions in olive oil until soft, then add chopped spinach and cook until wilted.

3. Remove from heat and let cool slightly. Stir in feta, ricotta, egg, salt, and pepper.

4. Brush a baking dish with olive oil and layer phyllo dough, brushing each sheet with oil.

5. Add spinach mixture, then top with more phyllo dough.

6. Bake for 30-35 minutes until golden and crispy.

Nutritional Facts: (Per serving)

- ❖ Calories: 250
- ❖ Fat: 16g
- ❖ Carbohydrates: 20g
- ❖ Fiber: 3g
- ❖ Protein: 7g

This traditional Greek spinach and cheese pie is a mouthwatering snack that combines crispy, flaky layers with a rich, savory filling. Perfect as an appetizer, snack, or light meal, it brings the flavors of Greece right to your table. Enjoy it fresh out of the oven for an unforgettable Mediterranean treat!

Recipe 30: Spinach and Feta Phyllo Purses

These spinach and feta phyllo purses are a delightful Mediterranean snack that combines the crispiness of phyllo dough with a flavorful spinach and feta filling. Perfect for serving as appetizers or a light meal, these savory pockets are easy to prepare and offer a burst of delicious Greek flavors in every bite.

Servings: 6

Prepping Time: 10 minutes

Cook Time: 25 minutes

Difficulty: Easy

Ingredients:

- ✓ 6 sheets of phyllo dough
- ✓ 2 cups fresh spinach, chopped
- ✓ 1/2 cup feta cheese, crumbled
- ✓ 1/4 cup ricotta cheese
- ✓ 1 tbsp olive oil
- ✓ 1 garlic clove, minced
- ✓ Salt and pepper to taste

Step-by-Step Preparation:

1. Preheat oven to 375°F (190°C).
2. Sauté garlic in olive oil, add spinach and cook until wilted. Remove from heat.
3. Stir in feta, ricotta, salt, and pepper.
4. Place one sheet of phyllo dough on a flat surface, brush with olive oil, and layer with another sheet.
5. Spoon the filling onto the center, fold the dough into a purse, and seal the edges.
6. Place on a baking sheet and bake for 20-25 minutes until golden brown.

Nutritional Facts: (Per serving)

- ❖ Calories: 220
- ❖ Fat: 14g
- ❖ Carbohydrates: 18g
- ❖ Fiber: 3g
- ❖ Protein: 7g

These spinach and feta phyllo purses are a fantastic Mediterranean snack that's both savory and satisfying. The crispy phyllo dough combined with the creamy, tangy filling makes each bite a flavorful experience. Serve them as appetizers at your next gathering, or enjoy them for a light, delicious meal!

Chapter 04: Sea-Inspired Snacks

←——————————————————————————————→

Recipe 31: Fried Crunchy Peeled Shrimps

Fried crunchy peeled shrimp with parsley, fried green chili pepper, and lemon, seasoned with salt, pepper, and spices, alongside grilled unpeeled shrimp with colorful bell pepper slices and sauce, is a delicious Mediterranean-inspired snack. This vibrant dish offers a burst of flavor while being simple to prepare and perfect for sharing.

Servings: 4

Prepping Time: 15 minutes

Cook Time: 10 minutes

Difficulty: Easy

Ingredients:

- ✓ 1 lb peeled shrimp
- ✓ 1/2 cup fresh parsley, chopped
- ✓ 2 green chili peppers, chopped
- ✓ 1 lemon, sliced
- ✓ Salt and pepper, to taste
- ✓ 1 tsp paprika
- ✓ 1 tsp garlic powder
- ✓ 1 tbsp olive oil
- ✓ 1 lb unpeeled shrimp
- ✓ 1 red bell pepper, sliced
- ✓ 1 yellow bell pepper, sliced
- ✓ 2 tbsp Mediterranean-style sauce (yogurt or tahini-based)

Step-by-Step Preparation:

1. Heat olive oil in a frying pan over medium-high heat.
2. Add peeled shrimp, parsley, green chili, and lemon slices. Season with salt, pepper, paprika, and garlic powder. Fry for 4-5 minutes until crispy.
3. In another pan, grill the unpeeled shrimp with bell pepper slices for 3-4 minutes, turning until cooked through.
4. Plate both shrimp preparations and drizzle with Mediterranean sauce.
5. Serve immediately with extra lemon wedges for garnish.

Nutritional Facts (Per serving):

- ❖ Calories: 220
- ❖ Protein: 28g
- ❖ Carbs: 10g
- ❖ Fat: 9g
- ❖ Fiber: 3g
- ❖ Sodium: 600mg

This Mediterranean-inspired snack is perfect for any occasion, offering a healthy, flavorful option that's easy to prepare. Ideal for a light lunch or appetizer, the combination of crispy shrimp, vibrant peppers, and tangy sauce will leave you craving more!

Recipe 32: Pizza in a Cone With Shrimps

Pizza in a cone with shrimp, zucchini, basil, and cheese offers a fun twist on traditional pizza. This Mediterranean-inspired snack is full of flavor and perfect for a casual meal or party treat. The crispy cone filled with savory shrimp, veggies, and melted cheese makes for a delightful bite that's both satisfying and healthy.

Servings: 4

Prepping Time: 20 minutes

Cook Time: 15 minutes

Difficulty: Medium

Ingredients:

- ✓ 1 lb shrimp, peeled and deveined
- ✓ 1 medium zucchini, thinly sliced
- ✓ 1/4 cup fresh basil, chopped
- ✓ 1 cup shredded mozzarella cheese
- ✓ 4 pizza cones (available in stores or made with pizza dough)
- ✓ 2 tbsp olive oil
- ✓ 1 tsp dried oregano
- ✓ Salt and pepper to taste

Step-by-Step Preparation:

1. Preheat the oven to 400°F (200°C).

2. Heat olive oil in a pan over medium heat. Add shrimp, zucchini, salt, pepper, and oregano. Sauté for 3-4 minutes until shrimp are cooked through and zucchini is tender.

3. Fill each pizza cone with the shrimp and zucchini mixture. Top with chopped basil and shredded mozzarella cheese.

4. Place the filled cones on a baking sheet and bake for 10 minutes, or until the cheese is melted and golden.

5. Serve hot, garnished with extra basil or a drizzle of olive oil if desired.

Nutritional Facts (Per serving):

- ❖ Calories: 280
- ❖ Protein: 20g
- ❖ Carbs: 18g
- ❖ Fat: 14g
- ❖ Fiber: 3g
- ❖ Sodium: 560mg

These pizza cones make an excellent snack or light meal. They combine the freshest Mediterranean flavors in a convenient, portable cone form, providing a perfect balance of protein and veggies. Enjoy this sea-inspired dish as a unique and flavorful treat!

Recipe 33: Deep-Fried Calamari Rings

Deep-fried calamari rings are a crispy, golden Mediterranean delight. This simple yet savory snack features tender squid coated in a light, crispy batter, making it perfect for dipping in your favorite sauce. Ideal for seafood lovers, these calamari rings are sure to become a favorite at your next gathering or as an appetizer.

Servings: 4

Prepping Time: 15 minutes

Cook Time: 5 minutes

Difficulty: Easy

Ingredients:

- ✓ 1 lb fresh calamari rings
- ✓ 1/2 cup all-purpose flour
- ✓ 1/2 tsp paprika
- ✓ 1/2 tsp garlic powder
- ✓ 1/4 tsp salt
- ✓ 1/4 tsp black pepper
- ✓ 1/2 cup breadcrumbs
- ✓ 1 egg, beaten
- ✓ Vegetable oil for frying
- ✓ Lemon wedges for serving

Step-by-Step Preparation:

1. In a shallow bowl, mix flour, paprika, garlic powder, salt, and pepper.

2. Dredge calamari rings in the flour mixture, then dip them into the beaten egg, and coat with breadcrumbs.

3. Heat oil in a deep pan or fryer to 375°F (190°C).

4. Fry calamari rings in batches for 2-3 minutes or until golden and crispy.

5. Drain on paper towels and serve immediately with lemon wedges.

Nutritional Facts (Per serving):

- ❖ Calories: 250
- ❖ Protein: 20g
- ❖ Carbs: 22g
- ❖ Fat: 12g
- ❖ Fiber: 1g
- ❖ Sodium: 650mg

These crispy calamari rings make a delicious Mediterranean-inspired snack or appetizer. Serve them with a side of marinara sauce or aioli for extra flavor. Light, satisfying, and full of flavor, this dish brings the taste of the sea right to your table!

Recipe 34: Fried Shrimps With Parsley

Fried shrimp with parsley, fried green chili pepper, and lemon is a Mediterranean-inspired snack that's packed with flavor. The crispy texture of the shrimp, combined with the zesty seasoning and the kick from the green chili, makes this dish irresistible. Perfect for seafood lovers, it's a quick and easy treat to enjoy at any time.

Servings: 4

Prepping Time: 15 minutes

Cook Time: 10 minutes

Difficulty: Easy

Ingredients:

- ✓ 1 lb peeled shrimp
- ✓ 2 tbsp fresh parsley, chopped
- ✓ 2 green chili peppers, chopped
- ✓ 1 lemon, sliced
- ✓ Salt and pepper, to taste
- ✓ 1 tsp paprika
- ✓ 1 tsp garlic powder
- ✓ 1/2 cup flour for coating
- ✓ Vegetable oil for frying

Step-by-Step Preparation:

1. In a shallow bowl, mix flour, salt, pepper, paprika, and garlic powder.
2. Dredge the shrimp in the flour mixture, ensuring they're evenly coated.
3. Heat oil in a frying pan over medium-high heat.
4. Add shrimp to the pan and fry for 2-3 minutes until golden and crispy.
5. Add chopped green chili peppers and parsley in the last minute of frying.
6. Remove shrimp and place on paper towels to drain excess oil.
7. Serve with lemon slices for a tangy finish.

Nutritional Facts (Per serving):

- ❖ Calories: 230
- ❖ Protein: 25g
- ❖ Carbs: 14g
- ❖ Fat: 10g
- ❖ Fiber: 2g
- ❖ Sodium: 570mg

These crispy fried shrimp with a tangy citrus twist are perfect as an appetizer or light snack. Bursting with flavor and quick to prepare, they offer a satisfying crunch and a hit of spice. Enjoy this Mediterranean delicacy with a refreshing drink on the side!

Recipe 35: King Prawns Battered in Panko Raincoat

King prawns battered in a crispy panko "raincoat" served with soy sauce and sesame seeds make for a delicious Mediterranean-inspired snack. This flavorful dish combines the light crunch of panko with the richness of prawns, balanced perfectly by the savory soy sauce. A quick and satisfying treat that's sure to please any seafood lover.

Servings: 4

Prepping Time: 10 minutes

Cook Time: 5 minutes

Difficulty: Easy

Ingredients:

- ✓ 1 lb king prawns, peeled and deveined
- ✓ 1 cup panko breadcrumbs
- ✓ 1 egg, beaten
- ✓ 1/4 cup flour
- ✓ Salt and pepper to taste
- ✓ 2 tbsp sesame seeds
- ✓ 1/4 cup soy sauce
- ✓ 1 tbsp olive oil for frying

Step-by-Step Preparation:

1. Season the prawns with salt and pepper.
2. Dredge prawns in flour, dip in the beaten egg, and coat with panko breadcrumbs.
3. Heat olive oil in a frying pan over medium heat.
4. Fry prawns for 2-3 minutes per side, until golden and crispy.
5. In a small bowl, combine soy sauce and sesame seeds.
6. Serve the prawns hot with the dipping sauce on the side.

Nutritional Facts (Per serving):

- ❖ Calories: 200
- ❖ Protein: 22g
- ❖ Carbs: 14g
- ❖ Fat: 8g
- ❖ Fiber: 2g
- ❖ Sodium: 600mg

These panko-battered king prawns offer a crunchy, savory bite with the perfect balance of flavors. Paired with soy sauce and sesame seeds, they make for a quick, easy, and indulgent Mediterranean snack that's perfect for any occasion. Enjoy these crispy delights fresh from the pan!

Recipe 36: Spanish Seafood Dish Chipirones, Battered Squid

Chipirones, a traditional Spanish seafood dish featuring battered squid, is a delicious Mediterranean-inspired snack. Crispy on the outside, tender on the inside, and served with a cold beer, it makes the perfect appetizer or light meal. This dish offers a great combination of textures and flavors, sure to impress seafood lovers.

Servings: 4

Cook Time: 5 minutes

Prepping Time: 15 minutes

Difficulty: Easy

Ingredients:

- ✓ 1 lb small squid (chipirones), cleaned and patted dry
- ✓ 1/2 cup flour
- ✓ 1 tsp paprika
- ✓ 1/2 tsp salt
- ✓ 1/4 tsp black pepper
- ✓ 1/2 cup cold beer
- ✓ Vegetable oil for frying
- ✓ Lemon wedges for serving

Step-by-Step Preparation:

1. In a bowl, mix flour, paprika, salt, and pepper.
2. Dredge the squid in the flour mixture, coating evenly.
3. Gradually add cold beer to the flour mixture to create a light batter.
4. Heat vegetable oil in a frying pan over medium-high heat.
5. Dip the battered squid into the hot oil and fry for 2-3 minutes, until golden brown and crispy.
6. Remove squid and place on paper towels to drain excess oil.
7. Serve with lemon wedges and a cold beer for the perfect pairing.

Nutritional Facts (Per serving):

- ❖ Calories: 220
- ❖ Protein: 18g
- ❖ Carbs: 15g
- ❖ Fat: 12g
- ❖ Fiber: 1g
- ❖ Sodium: 650mg

These crispy battered squid pieces are the perfect Mediterranean snack to pair with your favorite drink. Light, crunchy, and full of flavor, chipirones make for a satisfying treat that's perfect for casual gatherings or as an appetizer to share with friends. Enjoy this simple, tasty dish!

Recipe 37: Fried Fish Sticks With Fresh Vegetables

Fried fish sticks with fresh vegetables, tomatoes, peppers, and coriander offer a healthy, flavorful Mediterranean-inspired snack. The crispy fish, paired with a vibrant mix of vegetables, creates the perfect balance of textures and tastes. This quick and easy dish is great for lunch or a light appetizer, bringing the flavors of the sea right to your table.

Servings: 4

Prepping Time: 15 minutes

Cook Time: 10 minutes

Difficulty: Easy

Ingredients:

- ✓ 1 lb white fish fillets (cod, haddock, or tilapia), cut into strips
- ✓ 1/2 cup flour
- ✓ 1 egg, beaten
- ✓ 1/2 cup breadcrumbs
- ✓ 2 tbsp olive oil
- ✓ 1 tomato, diced
- ✓ 1 red bell pepper, diced
- ✓ 1/4 cup fresh coriander, chopped
- ✓ Salt and pepper to taste

Step-by-Step Preparation:

1. Season the fish strips with salt and pepper.
2. Dredge fish strips in flour, dip in the beaten egg, and coat with breadcrumbs.
3. Heat olive oil in a frying pan over medium heat.
4. Fry the fish sticks for 2-3 minutes per side, until golden brown and crispy.
5. In a separate bowl, combine diced tomatoes, bell pepper, and chopped coriander.
6. Serve the fried fish sticks with the fresh vegetable salad on the side.

Nutritional Facts (Per serving):

- ❖ Calories: 280
- ❖ Protein: 25g
- ❖ Carbs: 18g
- ❖ Fat: 14g
- ❖ Fiber: 4g
- ❖ Sodium: 480mg

These fried fish sticks with fresh vegetables are the ideal Mediterranean-inspired snack for any occasion. Crisp and satisfying, paired with a refreshing mix of tomatoes, peppers, and coriander, they make for a delicious and healthy treat. Perfect for a quick lunch or appetizer, enjoy the flavors of the Mediterranean in every bite!

Recipe 38: Mixed Fried Seafood

Mixed fried seafood with shrimp, squid, and baby octopus served with creamy mayonnaise sauce is a Mediterranean-inspired snack that's full of flavor. Crispy on the outside and tender on the inside, this dish brings together the best of the sea in a delightful, bite-sized form, perfect for sharing with friends or enjoying a light meal.

Servings: 4

Cook Time: 8 minutes

Prepping Time: 20 minutes

Difficulty: Easy

Ingredients:

- ✓ 1/2 lb shrimp, peeled and deveined
- ✓ 1/2 lb squid, cleaned and sliced
- ✓ 1/2 lb baby octopus, cleaned
- ✓ 1/2 cup flour
- ✓ 1/2 cup cornstarch
- ✓ 1 tsp paprika
- ✓ Salt and pepper to taste
- ✓ Vegetable oil for frying
- ✓ 1/2 cup mayonnaise
- ✓ 1 tsp lemon juice

Step-by-Step Preparation:

1. Season the seafood with salt, pepper, and paprika.
2. In a bowl, combine flour, cornstarch, and a pinch of salt.
3. Dredge shrimp, squid, and octopus in the flour mixture, coating them evenly.
4. Heat vegetable oil in a frying pan over medium-high heat.
5. Fry the seafood in batches for 2-3 minutes until golden and crispy.
6. For the sauce, mix mayonnaise and lemon juice in a bowl.
7. Serve the fried seafood hot with the creamy mayo sauce on the side.

Nutritional Facts (Per serving):

- ❖ Calories: 270
- ❖ Protein: 25g
- ❖ Carbs: 20g
- ❖ Fat: 15g
- ❖ Fiber: 2g
- ❖ Sodium: 500mg

This mixed-fried seafood is the perfect Mediterranean snack, offering a crispy, flavorful combination of shrimp, squid, and baby octopus. Paired with a tangy mayonnaise sauce, it's a satisfying dish that's easy to make and even easier to enjoy. Ideal for gatherings or as a delicious treat anytime!

Recipe 39: Chopped Squid Breaded

Chopped squid breaded with flour and egg, then fried in olive oil, offers a Mediterranean-inspired snack that's both crispy and tender. The light batter and fresh lemon seasoning bring out the natural flavors of the squid, making this dish a perfect appetizer or light meal. Enjoy this quick and delicious seafood treat, ideal for seafood lovers!

Servings: 4

Prepping Time: 15 minutes

Cook Time: 5 minutes

Difficulty: Easy

Ingredients:

- ✓ 1 lb squid, cleaned and chopped
- ✓ 1/2 cup flour
- ✓ 1 egg, beaten
- ✓ 1/4 cup olive oil
- ✓ Salt and pepper to taste
- ✓ 1 lemon, sliced

Step-by-Step Preparation:

1. Season the chopped squid with salt and pepper.
2. Dredge the squid in flour, dip it in the beaten egg, and coat again in flour.
3. Heat olive oil in a frying pan over medium-high heat.
4. Fry the squid for 2-3 minutes, until golden and crispy.
5. Remove the squid and place on paper towels to drain excess oil.
6. Serve with fresh lemon slices to squeeze over the top.

Nutritional Facts (Per serving):

- ❖ Calories: 210
- ❖ Protein: 20g
- ❖ Carbs: 15g
- ❖ Fat: 12g
- ❖ Fiber: 1g
- ❖ Sodium: 400mg

These crispy, golden squid bites are a perfect Mediterranean-inspired snack that's easy to prepare and full of flavor. The addition of lemon enhances the dish, making it fresh and vibrant. Ideal for any seafood lover, this dish brings the tastes of the Mediterranean straight to your table!

Recipe 40: Open Shrimps Empanadas With Gratin Cheese

Open shrimp empanadas with gratin cheese offer a Mediterranean twist on a classic snack. Filled with juicy shrimp and topped with melted cheese, these empanadas are baked until golden and crispy. Ideal as an appetizer or light meal, they are rich in flavor and perfect for seafood lovers looking for a savory treat.

Servings: 4

Prepping Time: 20 minutes

Cook Time: 15 minutes

Difficulty: Medium

Ingredients:

- ✓ 1 lb shrimp, peeled and deveined
- ✓ 1 tbsp olive oil
- ✓ 1/2 onion, finely chopped
- ✓ 1/2 cup grated cheese (preferably mozzarella or cheddar)
- ✓ 1/4 cup fresh parsley, chopped
- ✓ 4 empanada dough rounds (store-bought or homemade)
- ✓ 1 egg, beaten
- ✓ Salt and pepper to taste

Step-by-Step Preparation:

1. Preheat the oven to 375°F (190°C).
2. Heat olive oil in a pan and sauté onions until soft. Add shrimp and cook for 3-4 minutes until pink. Season with salt and pepper.
3. Remove from heat and stir in chopped parsley.
4. Place the empanada dough rounds on a baking sheet.
5. Spoon the shrimp mixture onto the center of each round and top with grated cheese.
6. Fold the dough edges to form an open pocket. Brush with beaten egg for a golden finish.
7. Bake for 12-15 minutes or until golden brown and crispy.

Nutritional Facts (Per serving):

- ❖ Calories: 300
- ❖ Protein: 25g
- ❖ Carbs: 18g
- ❖ Fat: 18g
- ❖ Fiber: 2g
- ❖ Sodium: 600mg

These open shrimp empanadas with gratin cheese are a delicious fusion of Mediterranean flavors in a crispy, cheesy package. They're perfect for any occasion—whether served as an appetizer or a main dish. Indulge in the rich, savory flavors of shrimp and cheese with this easy-to-make, crowd-pleasing snack!

Chapter 05: Sweet Mediterranean Treats

Recipe 41: Sweet Baklava Pastry

Sweet Baklava Pastry is a delicious Mediterranean treat made with crispy layers of filo dough, filled with chopped nuts, and drenched in honey or syrup. Perfect for a snack or dessert, it offers a balance of rich flavors and a satisfying crunch in every bite.

Servings: 8

Prepping Time: 20 minutes

Cook Time: 40 minutes

Difficulty: Medium

Ingredients:

- ✓ 16 sheets of filo dough
- ✓ 1 cup mixed nuts (walnuts, pistachios, almonds)
- ✓ 1/2 cup unsalted butter, melted
- ✓ 1/2 cup honey
- ✓ 1/2 cup water
- ✓ 1 cup granulated sugar
- ✓ 1 teaspoon lemon juice
- ✓ 1 teaspoon ground cinnamon

Step-by-Step Preparation:

1. Preheat your oven to 350°F (175°C).
2. Brush a 9x13-inch baking dish with melted butter.
3. Place a sheet of filo dough in the dish and brush with more melted butter. Repeat layering 8 sheets.
4. Chop the mixed nuts finely and sprinkle evenly over the filo dough.
5. Layer another 8 sheets of filo dough, brushing each with melted butter.
6. Cut the baklava into diamond or square shapes before baking.
7. Bake in the preheated oven for 30-40 minutes or until golden brown and crisp.
8. While baking, prepare the syrup: Combine honey, water, sugar, and lemon juice in a saucepan and simmer for 10 minutes.
9. Pour the hot syrup evenly over the baked baklava and allow to cool completely before serving.

Nutritional Facts: (Per serving)

- ❖ Calories: 260
- ❖ Total Fat: 14g
- ❖ Saturated Fat: 3g
- ❖ Cholesterol: 10mg
- ❖ Sodium: 25mg
- ❖ Total Carbohydrates: 31g
- ❖ Dietary Fiber: 3g
- ❖ Sugars: 22g
- ❖ Protein: 4g

This Sweet Baklava Pastry makes a perfect treat for any occasion, combining rich, nutty flavors with a sticky sweetness. Try it out and enjoy this Mediterranean delight with your loved ones!

Recipe 42: Fried Halloumi Cheese Sticks

Fried halloumi cheese sticks with tomato sauce are a savory Mediterranean snack that offers the perfect combination of crispy, golden-brown cheese and tangy, rich tomato sauce. This easy-to-make treat is perfect for satisfying cravings or serving as an appetizer.

Servings: 4

Prepping Time: 10 minutes

Cook Time: 10 minutes

Difficulty: Easy

Ingredients:

- ✓ 200g halloumi cheese
- ✓ 1/4 cup all-purpose flour
- ✓ 1/4 cup breadcrumbs
- ✓ 1/4 cup grated Parmesan cheese
- ✓ 1 egg, beaten
- ✓ 1 tablespoon olive oil (for frying)
- ✓ 1/2 cup tomato sauce
- ✓ 1 teaspoon dried oregano
- ✓ Fresh parsley for garnish

Step-by-Step Preparation:

1. Cut the halloumi cheese into thick strips.
2. In one bowl, mix flour, breadcrumbs, and Parmesan cheese. In another bowl, whisk the egg.
3. Dip each halloumi strip into the egg, then coat with the breadcrumb mixture.
4. Heat olive oil in a frying pan over medium heat. Fry the halloumi strips until golden brown, about 2-3 minutes on each side.
5. While the cheese is frying, heat the tomato sauce in a small saucepan and stir in oregano.
6. Remove the fried halloumi from the pan and drain on a paper towel.
7. Serve the fried halloumi with the warm tomato sauce and garnish with fresh parsley.

Nutritional Facts: (Per serving)

- ❖ Calories: 290
- ❖ Total Fat: 22g
- ❖ Saturated Fat: 10g
- ❖ Cholesterol: 45mg
- ❖ Sodium: 500mg
- ❖ Total Carbohydrates: 12g
- ❖ Dietary Fiber: 1g
- ❖ Sugars: 3g
- ❖ Protein: 17g

These fried halloumi cheese sticks are crispy, cheesy, and absolutely irresistible. Serve them with tangy tomato sauce for the perfect Mediterranean-inspired snack that everyone will love!

Recipe 43: Greek Pastry Bougatsa

Greek Bougatsa is a delicious pastry made with crispy phyllo dough and a creamy semolina custard filling. This sweet Mediterranean treat offers a perfect balance of textures and flavors, making it ideal for breakfast or dessert.

Servings: 8

Cook Time: 40 minutes

Prepping Time: 20 minutes

Difficulty: Medium

Ingredients:

- ✓ 12 sheets of phyllo dough
- ✓ 1 cup semolina
- ✓ 2 cups milk
- ✓ 1/2 cup granulated sugar
- ✓ 1 teaspoon vanilla extract
- ✓ 2 large eggs
- ✓ 1/4 cup unsalted butter, melted
- ✓ Powdered sugar for dusting

Step-by-Step Preparation:

1. Preheat the oven to 350°F (175°C).
2. In a saucepan, heat the milk over medium heat. Gradually add semolina and sugar, whisking constantly until the mixture thickens.
3. Remove from heat and stir in vanilla extract and eggs, one at a time, to form a smooth custard.
4. Brush a baking dish with melted butter and layer 6 sheets of phyllo dough, brushing each with more butter.
5. Spread the semolina custard over the phyllo dough.
6. Cover with the remaining phyllo dough sheets, buttering each layer.
7. Bake for 35-40 minutes or until golden brown and crispy.
8. Let the Bougatsa cool slightly, then dust with powdered sugar before serving.

Nutritional Facts: (Per serving)

- ❖ Calories: 310
- ❖ Total Fat: 18g
- ❖ Saturated Fat: 6g
- ❖ Cholesterol: 80mg
- ❖ Sodium: 50mg
- ❖ Total Carbohydrates: 33g
- ❖ Dietary Fiber: 1g
- ❖ Sugars: 16g
- ❖ Protein: 6g

Bougatsa is a wonderful treat that brings the flavors of Greece right to your table. Whether as a breakfast delight or a sweet dessert, it's sure to impress with its flaky layers and creamy filling!

Recipe 44: Stuffed Croquettes Iberico Ham and Cheese

Delicious stuffed croquettes with Iberico ham and cheese are a savory Mediterranean snack that's crispy on the outside and melty on the inside. These indulgent bites are perfect for parties or a comforting treat, offering the rich flavors of Iberico ham combined with gooey cheese.

Servings: 4

Prepping Time: 15 minutes

Cook Time: 15 minutes

Difficulty: Medium

Ingredients:

- ✓ 1 cup Iberico ham, finely chopped
- ✓ 1 cup cheese (Manchego or mozzarella), grated
- ✓ 1/2 cup all-purpose flour
- ✓ 1/2 cup milk
- ✓ 1/4 cup unsalted butter
- ✓ 1 egg, beaten
- ✓ 1 cup breadcrumbs
- ✓ Olive oil for frying
- ✓ Salt and pepper to taste

Step-by-Step Preparation:

1. In a saucepan, melt the butter over medium heat. Add the flour and cook, stirring, for 1-2 minutes to form a roux.
2. Gradually whisk in the milk and cook until the mixture thickens about 3 minutes.
3. Stir in the chopped Iberico ham, grated cheese, salt, and pepper. Allow the mixture to cool slightly.
4. Shape the cooled mixture into small croquette-sized cylinders.
5. Dip each croquette into the beaten egg, then coat it with breadcrumbs.
6. Heat olive oil in a pan over medium heat and fry the croquettes until golden brown, about 3-4 minutes on each side.
7. Remove the croquettes and drain on paper towels before serving.

Nutritional Facts: (Per serving)

- ❖ Calories: 300
- ❖ Total Fat: 18g
- ❖ Saturated Fat: 8g
- ❖ Cholesterol: 45mg
- ❖ Sodium: 550mg
- ❖ Total Carbohydrates: 25g
- ❖ Dietary Fiber: 1g
- ❖ Sugars: 2g
- ❖ Protein: 15g

These Iberico ham and cheese croquettes are irresistible with their crispy coating and melted filling. Serve them hot for a perfect Mediterranean snack that's sure to be a hit at any gathering!

Recipe 45: Sweet Italian Cookies

Sweet Italian Taralli cookies are a delightful Mediterranean treat made with white wine, sugar, olive oil, eggs, and flour. These crunchy, slightly sweet cookies are perfect for snacking with a cup of tea or coffee and bring a taste of Italy to your home.

Servings: 12

Cook Time: 25 minutes

Prepping Time: 15 minutes

Difficulty: Easy

Ingredients:

- ✓ 2 cups all-purpose flour
- ✓ 1/2 cup white wine
- ✓ 1/4 cup olive oil
- ✓ 1/4 cup sugar
- ✓ 1 egg
- ✓ 1 teaspoon vanilla extract
- ✓ A pinch of salt

Step-by-Step Preparation:

1. Preheat the oven to 350°F (175°C) and line a baking sheet with parchment paper.
2. In a large bowl, combine the flour, sugar, and salt.
3. In a separate bowl, whisk together the egg, white wine, olive oil, and vanilla extract.
4. Gradually add the wet ingredients to the dry ingredients, mixing until a dough forms.
5. Turn the dough out onto a floured surface and knead until smooth.
6. Roll the dough into small logs, about 3 inches long, and form into rings.
7. Place the rings on the baking sheet and bake for 20-25 minutes or until golden brown.
8. Allow the Taralli to cool before serving.

Nutritional Facts: (Per serving)

- ❖ Calories: 180
- ❖ Total Fat: 7g
- ❖ Saturated Fat: 1g
- ❖ Cholesterol: 20mg
- ❖ Sodium: 80mg
- ❖ Total Carbohydrates: 26g
- ❖ Dietary Fiber: 1g
- ❖ Sugars: 6g
- ❖ Protein: 3g

These Sweet Italian Taralli cookies are simple yet flavorful, offering a perfect balance of sweetness and crunch. Enjoy them as a delightful snack or dessert!

Recipe 46: Authentic Greek Fried Cheese

Saganaki, or fried feta cheese, is a mouthwatering Greek treat that's crispy on the outside, soft and creamy on the inside, and topped with honey and sesame seeds. This Mediterranean delight is perfect as a savory snack or appetizer, offering a perfect balance of sweet and salty flavors.

Servings: 4

Prepping Time: 10 minutes

Cook Time: 5 minutes

Difficulty: Easy

Ingredients:

- ✓ 200g feta cheese
- ✓ 2 tablespoons olive oil
- ✓ 1 tablespoon sesame seeds
- ✓ 1 tablespoon honey
- ✓ 1 tablespoon flour
- ✓ Freshly ground black pepper to taste
- ✓ Lemon wedges for serving (optional)

Step-by-Step Preparation:

1. Slice the feta cheese into thick squares or triangles.
2. Lightly coat the feta pieces in flour, shaking off any excess.
3. Heat olive oil in a pan over medium heat.
4. Fry the feta for 2-3 minutes on each side, until golden and crispy.
5. Once fried, transfer to a plate and drizzle with honey.
6. Sprinkle with sesame seeds and a dash of freshly ground black pepper.
7. Serve immediately with lemon wedges on the side for a refreshing kick.

Nutritional Facts: (Per serving)

- ❖ Calories: 250
- ❖ Total Fat: 18g
- ❖ Saturated Fat: 9g
- ❖ Cholesterol: 30mg
- ❖ Sodium: 700mg
- ❖ Total Carbohydrates: 9g
- ❖ Dietary Fiber: 1g
- ❖ Sugars: 5g
- ❖ Protein: 9g

This Authentic Greek Fried Cheese is a delightful fusion of crispy, creamy, and sweet flavors. Enjoy it as a savory snack or appetizer that brings a taste of Greece right to your table!

Recipe 47: Buffalo Wings Baked With Sweet Small Potatoes

Buffalo wings, crunchy and crispy, paired with sweet small potatoes, parsley, and green garlic leaves, offer a perfect balance of bold flavors and textures. This Mediterranean-inspired snack is not only delicious but also a healthier alternative to traditional fried wings, baked to perfection with a sweet and savory twist.

Servings: 4

Cook Time: 35 minutes

Prepping Time: 15 minutes

Difficulty: Medium

Ingredients:

- ✓ 12 chicken wings
- ✓ 2 small sweet potatoes, diced
- ✓ 2 tablespoons olive oil
- ✓ 1 tablespoon paprika
- ✓ 1 tablespoon garlic powder
- ✓ 1 teaspoon cayenne pepper
- ✓ Salt and pepper to taste
- ✓ 1/4 cup fresh parsley, chopped
- ✓ 2 green garlic leaves, finely chopped
- ✓ 1/4 cup buffalo sauce

Step-by-Step Preparation:

1. Preheat your oven to 400°F (200°C) and line a baking sheet with parchment paper.
2. Toss the chicken wings with olive oil, paprika, garlic powder, cayenne pepper, salt, and pepper. Arrange on one side of the baking sheet.
3. Toss the diced sweet potatoes with olive oil, salt, and pepper. Place on the other side of the baking sheet.
4. Bake for 25 minutes, flipping halfway through, until the wings are crispy and golden and the potatoes are tender.
5. Drizzle the buffalo sauce over the wings and return to the oven for another 5-10 minutes.
6. Once baked, sprinkle the wings and potatoes with chopped parsley and green garlic leaves before serving.

Nutritional Facts: (Per serving)

- ❖ Calories: 300
- ❖ Total Fat: 15g
- ❖ Saturated Fat: 2g
- ❖ Cholesterol: 70mg
- ❖ Sodium: 550mg
- ❖ Total Carbohydrates: 25g
- ❖ Dietary Fiber: 4g
- ❖ Sugars: 6g
- ❖ Protein: 20g

These Buffalo Wings with Sweet Potatoes are a flavorful and crispy snack, offering a perfect balance of spice, sweetness, and freshness. Enjoy this Mediterranean twist for your next treat!

Recipe 48: Phyllo-Wrapped Feta With Honey and Sesame Seeds

Phyllo-wrapped feta with honey and sesame seeds is a delicious Mediterranean treat that combines the crispy layers of phyllo dough with the creamy, salty feta and the sweetness of honey. This easy-to-make snack offers the perfect balance of textures and flavors.

Servings: 6

Prepping Time: 15 minutes

Cook Time: 20 minutes

Difficulty: Easy

Ingredients:

- ✓ 200g feta cheese
- ✓ 6 sheets of phyllo dough
- ✓ 2 tablespoons olive oil
- ✓ 1 tablespoon honey
- ✓ 1 tablespoon sesame seeds
- ✓ Fresh thyme (optional)

Step-by-Step Preparation:

1. Preheat the oven to 375°F (190°C) and line a baking sheet with parchment paper.
2. Slice the feta cheese into rectangles.
3. Lay one sheet of phyllo dough on a flat surface and brush with olive oil. Layer with another sheet and brush again.
4. Place a piece of feta on the phyllo dough and fold the dough around it to create a parcel.
5. Repeat with the remaining feta and phyllo dough sheets.
6. Place the wrapped feta on the baking sheet and bake for 15-20 minutes or until golden and crispy.
7. Drizzle honey over the baked phyllo parcels and sprinkle with sesame seeds. Garnish with fresh thyme if desired.

Nutritional Facts: (Per serving)

- ❖ Calories: 250
- ❖ Total Fat: 18g
- ❖ Saturated Fat: 7g
- ❖ Cholesterol: 30mg
- ❖ Sodium: 600mg
- ❖ Total Carbohydrates: 12g
- ❖ Dietary Fiber: 1g
- ❖ Sugars: 5g
- ❖ Protein: 8g

This Phyllo-wrapped feta with Honey and Sesame Seeds is a mouthwatering snack that offers a crispy exterior and a creamy, flavorful interior. Serve it warm for a delightful Mediterranean treat!

Recipe 49: Baked Camembert Brie

Baked Camembert brie with fresh rosemary and cranberry sauce is a decadent Mediterranean snack perfect for any occasion. The creamy cheese melts beautifully in the oven, while the fresh rosemary adds an aromatic touch, and the cranberry sauce provides a perfect sweet and tangy contrast.

Servings: 4

Prepping Time: 10 minutes

Cook Time: 20 minutes

Difficulty: Easy

Ingredients:

- ✓ 1 wheel of Camembert or Brie cheese
- ✓ 1 tablespoon fresh rosemary, chopped
- ✓ 1/4 cup cranberry sauce
- ✓ 1 tablespoon olive oil
- ✓ Salt and pepper to taste
- ✓ Fresh baguette or crackers for serving

Step-by-Step Preparation:

1. Preheat the oven to 350°F (175°C).
2. Place the Camembert or Brie cheese wheel in a small baking dish.
3. Drizzle olive oil over the cheese and sprinkle with fresh rosemary, salt, and pepper.
4. Bake for 15-20 minutes, until the cheese is soft and melted.
5. While baking, warm the cranberry sauce in a small pot over low heat.
6. Remove the cheese from the oven and top with warm cranberry sauce.
7. Serve with fresh baguette slices or crackers.

Nutritional Facts: (Per serving)

- ❖ Calories: 200
- ❖ Total Fat: 16g
- ❖ Saturated Fat: 8g
- ❖ Cholesterol: 30mg
- ❖ Sodium: 200mg
- ❖ Total Carbohydrates: 10g
- ❖ Dietary Fiber: 1g
- ❖ Sugars: 6g
- ❖ Protein: 8g

This Baked Camembert with Rosemary and Cranberry Sauce is a perfect blend of creamy, savory, and sweet flavors. Serve it warm for a luxurious Mediterranean-inspired snack that's sure to impress!

Recipe 50: Traditional Cretan Pekmezi Cookies

Cretan pekmezi cookies, or moustou koulouri, are a traditional Greek treat made with grape molasses and aromatic spices. These soft, slightly chewy cookies offer a delightful balance of sweetness and spice, capturing the essence of Mediterranean flavors in every bite.

Servings: 12

Prepping Time: 20 minutes

Cook Time: 25 minutes

Difficulty: Medium

Ingredients:

- ✓ 1 cup whole wheat flour
- ✓ 1/2 cup all-purpose flour
- ✓ 1/2 cup grape molasses (pekmezi)
- ✓ 1/4 cup olive oil
- ✓ 1 teaspoon ground cinnamon
- ✓ 1/2 teaspoon ground cloves
- ✓ 1/4 teaspoon baking soda
- ✓ Pinch of salt
- ✓ 1/4 cup chopped walnuts (optional)

Step-by-Step Preparation:

1. Preheat your oven to 350°F (175°C) and line a baking sheet with parchment paper.
2. In a bowl, mix the flour, cinnamon, cloves, baking soda, and salt.
3. In a separate bowl, combine the grape molasses and olive oil.
4. Gradually mix the wet ingredients into the dry ingredients, stirring until a dough forms.
5. If desired, fold in the chopped walnuts.
6. Shape the dough into small rounds or ovals and place them on the prepared baking sheet.
7. Bake for 20-25 minutes or until the edges are lightly golden.
8. Allow to cool on a wire rack before serving.

Nutritional Facts: (Per serving)

- ❖ Calories: 160
- ❖ Total Fat: 8g
- ❖ Saturated Fat: 1g
- ❖ Cholesterol: 0mg
- ❖ Sodium: 50mg
- ❖ Total Carbohydrates: 20g
- ❖ Dietary Fiber: 2g
- ❖ Sugars: 10g
- ❖ Protein: 2g

These Traditional Cretan Pekmezi Cookies are perfect with a cup of tea or coffee, offering a delightful taste of the Mediterranean in every bite. Enjoy this sweet, aromatic treat any time!

Conclusion

Thank you for choosing Delicious Mediterranean Diet Snacks Recipes Cookbook: Tasty Bites, Simple Steps, Colorful Photos! We hope this book has inspired you to incorporate more healthy, vibrant Mediterranean snacks into your daily routine. With 50 carefully selected recipes, you now have the perfect collection to create delicious, nutritious snacks that support your health goals without compromising on flavor.

What You've Discovered:

- ✓ **50 Authentic Recipes**: A wide variety of Mediterranean-inspired snacks perfect for any time of the day.
- ✓ **5 Chapters**:
    - ✓ **Classic Mediterranean Bites**: Timeless, savory options that never go out of style.
    - ✓ **Crunchy & Nutty Treats**: Satisfying snacks with the perfect crunch.
    - ✓ **Vegetable Delights**: Fresh, veggie-packed snacks for a healthy bite.
    - ✓ **Sea-Inspired Snacks**: Delicious seafood-based options to tempt your taste buds.
    - ✓ **Sweet Mediterranean Treats**: Guilt-free desserts that are both sweet and healthy.
- ✓ **Original, Colorful Photos**: Each recipe comes with a stunning photo to guide you and inspire your cooking.
- ✓ **Easy-to-Follow Instructions**: Simple and clear steps for effortless cooking.
- ✓ **Perfect Flavors**: Each recipe has been carefully crafted to ensure a balance of taste and nutrition.
- ✓ **No Grammar or Spelling Errors**: Professionally proofread for clarity and a seamless experience.

We hope Delicious Mediterranean Diet Snacks Recipes Cookbook becomes a go-to resource in your kitchen, helping you enjoy the vibrant flavors and health benefits of Mediterranean cuisine. May this cookbook empower you to create flavorful and wholesome snacks, enhancing your healthy eating journey.

Happy cooking and enjoy your Mediterranean-inspired snacks!

Made in United States
Troutdale, OR
04/13/2025